W9-BEU-788

What people have said about...

Wake up and smell the profit

"It should come with a health warning that it should not be read at bedtime, since you wont sleep after it, as your mind will be buzzing with great ideas."

Robert Bligh – Just Bean Espresso Bar

"A really fun read, full of proven ideas and sensible advice to make money but also enjoy your business at the same time. A must for anyone wanting to start a coffee bar and many operators would benefit from a read as well."

Steve Penk - UK National Co-Ordinator & Director of the Speciality Coffee Association of Europe

"A quite brilliant new book on cafe operation... sometimes all of us are lucky enough to learn from those who have turned their mistakes into practical experience, such as in this exceptional new book from Ireland's 'Coffee Boys', John Richardson and Hugh Gilmartin."

Ian Boughton – Coffee House Magazine

"Absolutely nobody should open a coffee shop without first reading this book. We have already incorporated it into our training program and manuals."

Se Gorman – Entrepreneur and National Barista Champion 2006 and 2007

howtobooks

Please send for a free copy of the latest catalogue:

How To Books
Spring Hill House, Spring Hill Road, Begbroke,
Oxford OX5 1RX, United Kingdom
email: info@howtobooks.co.uk
http://www.howtobooks.co.uk

Wake up
and smell the

52 profit

GUARANTEED WAYS...

...TO MAKE MORE MONEY IN YOUR COFFEE BUSINESS

John Richardson & Hugh Gilmartin

howto**books**

Published by How To Books Ltd,
Spring Hill House, Spring Hill Road,
Begbroke, Oxford OX5 1RX, United Kingdom
Tel: (01865) 375794. Fax: (01865) 379162
info@howtobooks.co.uk
www.howtobooks.co.uk

How To Books greatly reduce the carbon footprint of their books by sourcing
their typesetting and printing in the UK.

All rights reserved. No part of this work may be reproduced or stored in an
information retrieval system (other than for purposes of review) without the
express permission of the publisher in writing.

The rights of John Richardson and Hugh Gilmartin to be identified as authors
of this work have been asserted by them in accordance with the Copyright,
Designs and Patents Act 1988.

© 2008 John Richardson and Hugh Gilmartin

First edition 2006
Second edition 2008

British Library Cataloguing in Publication Data
A catalogue record for this book is available from the British Library.

ISBN: 978-1-84528-334-6

Cover design by Baseline Arts Ltd, Oxford
Produced for How To Books by Deer Park Productions, Tavistock
Typeset by Baseline Arts Ltd, Oxford
Printed and bound by Cromwell Press Ltd, Trowbridge, Wiltshire

NOTE: The material contained in this book is set out in good faith for general
guidance and no liability can be accepted for loss or expense incurred as a
result of relying in particular circumstances on statements made in the book.
Laws and regulations are complex and liable to change, and readers should
check the current position with the relevant authorities before making personal
arrangements.

Contents

This book is dedicated to Vilfredo Pareto.

Pareto's key idea was that 80% of your profit is achieved by 20% of what you do. It is this concept that has inspired both of us to figure out exactly what that 20% is.

John Richardson by Hugh Gilmartin

I first met Johnnie when he was growing
what became at the time the largest
sandwich business in Ireland. I got to know him pretty well over
the years as he opened several new enterprises and I supplied him
with a lot of coffee in a number of diverse and award winning
businesses.

As we progressed I discovered that, despite his business degree and
marketing qualifications, he had learnt everything he knew about
running food and beverage businesses not from textbooks but
from real experience. A lot of "real world" trial and error as well as a
fair few mistakes along the way. His advice was always based on
genuine experience – never from fancy theories.

As I started 'modeling' John's advice with my customers, I began to
see just how much of what he said made sense and I started to
notice an improvement in their bottom lines. Much of the advice is
actually common sense, but the organised fashion in which it was
presented made an enormous difference. I began to realise that, in
the world of business, common sense was indeed uncommon.

John has been, and still is, involved in some of the most successful
sandwich & coffee bars, café's, and turnkey consultancy projects in
Northern Ireland and is an expert in marketing and financial
business modeling. John currently spends most of his time helping
his international client base increase their profitability in their coffee
related businesses.

Hugh Gilmartin by John Richardson

When I first met Hugo fifteen years ago, he was clearly so much more than just a coffee salesman. His enormous passion and knowledge about coffee meant that I immediately felt I wanted him to be the man to supply me with a coffee "solution" for my own business. His business has diversified over the years but he still maintains an almost messianic passion for great coffee and always couples this with a desire to help his customers make more money.

More than any other supplier I've come across in the hospitality business, Hugh always has the customer's needs foremost in his mind. He knows that a lasting relationship can only be built by focusing on what the customer wants and needs long term – not the quick short-term sale.

This attitude means that he has now created what is comfortably the largest coffee business in Northern Ireland. He has a team of coffee specialists who have been with him for years and they provide total coffee solutions to their diverse customer base. Like Hugh, they pay obsessive attention to making what they sell taste great.

Hugh is well known in international coffee business circles. He speaks at conferences in Europe & the US, and is a board member of The Specialty Coffee Association of Europe.

Introduction

This book is not intended to be an exhaustive manual or a textbook on running a coffee business. It is a, hopefully entertaining, wake-up call to the sometimes harsh realities of making money in the business of coffee.

Whilst the tone may be light there is an underlying serious message. That running a coffee business, of any type, is ultimately about making profit. Passion and creating great products are very important but if you don't focus on profit you'll have no business to be passionate about. Every one of the 52 (+1) ways is directly focused at helping you make more money in your business.

John Richardson and Hugh Gilmartin have between them nearly forty years experience in the hospitality industry. Forty years of managing, owning, supplying and consulting to a vast array of businesses. From single site espresso bars to Michelin starred restaurants and hotel chains there is almost no section of the market that they aren't familiar with.

In this book they bring together their favourite stories and wake-up calls from this experience. The experience of dealing with all kinds of customers and people related directly and indirectly to the business of coffee.

The book is intended to be a "dip into" type of guide that you can refer to in a moment of spare time. We recognise that time is tight but if you read just one idea a week for the next year and apply just a few of them then you cannot fail to see an increase in your profits.

Don't forget to give us feedback and perhaps wake us up to a few new ideas and comment via email or The Coffeeboys blog. Tell us what works for you and what doesn't and join our Coffee Club consisting of other like minded coffee people who realise that first and foremost it's a business and then it's your passion.

Okay let's go…

1. It's all about the money – the good news!

The café business (in all its different forms) really is a great way to make money. It isn't easy, but if you play the game properly and work hard you really can make a lot of money with a great lifestyle to go along with it. But there are some rules that you need to be aware of. **Break these rules at your peril.**

So what are these rules? How should a perfect coffee shop work? What exactly should you be expecting from your business financially?

Well, the figures vary for a number of reasons, but unless you are paying huge rent (more than 10% of your turnover) then ideally you don't want your wage bill and food cost to be more than 65% of your total sales (after any VAT or sales tax). The goal should ideally be 60% as a total for these two combined. How this breaks down between them is entirely based on the model you operate. A coffee shop which makes all its own food from raw ingredients will be aiming for a food cost (total including drinks) of about 25% and a wage cost of about 35%. A coffee shop which buys in most of what it is selling should be aiming for about 35% food cost and 25% wage cost, since you need less staff to prepare the food and obviously won't be able to buy as cheaply because you need to give the food producer some margin.

This leaves you with 35 – 40% contribution to overhead. If your rent and rates are approximately 10% of your turnover then you are left with 25 – 30% for general running expenses and depreciation.

So if it all hangs together, you should be able to put 15% to the bottom line – more if you are working hands on in the business yourself.

This 15%-20% is your target and you must know the numbers for your business. That means you should be able to make about £30,000 on net turnover of about £200,000, but be aware that this should be more if you are working there yourself. Always work your figures out based on having paid yourself a reasonable salary – but only if you physically work there. Not if you are sitting at home eating cake or hacking your way round the golf course in an interesting pair of trousers.

Rent, rates and general overheads are relatively fixed but you do need to make sure you have a tight rein on them. The big areas to watch weekly are your food cost and wage cost. We'll say it again – make sure you know these weekly. If you can run a really tight ship then 20% is very achievable – more if you're clever. Work out where you are and create a clear target and plan for where you want to be.

And don't forget….
Know your food cost and wage cost weekly.

2. It's all about the money – the bad news!

Sounds obvious but it really, really isn't. The number one issue that we deal with is clients who will not accept, either consciously or subconsciously, that they are running a business. Of course heaven forbid we would be lumping you into that category, but let us indulge ourselves for a minute. **You simply have to grasp this concept.**

Going bankrupt or out of business in any way is a horrible, humiliating thing. It is the kind of event that you really want to avoid. We both know from bitter personal experience. Time after time we still see it, year in and year out. Clients and friends who just won't accept that running a food or coffee business is about money and not some wonderful lifestyle choice.

Wake up to the reality of making money...

"It's a kind of spiritual snobbery that makes people think they can be happy without money."
Albert Camus

Let us just put a few possibilities to you. A little list of horrible things that happen if you don't keep the money thing right at the forefront of your mind.

- Creditors beating down your door and trying to find your home address.

- Having to tell staff they no longer have jobs.

- Having those same staff that you paid for years get cross with you because you messed up and they have no job.

- Slimy, oily food reps, who you tolerated for years and used to schmooze you, becoming arrogant and rude, asking for money.

- Pitying looks from friends and family.

- Having to put up with those same friends and family telling you that you now must get a job and maybe "running a business just wasn't right for you".

- Having cars repossessed.

- Sitting in front of creditors at a meeting whilst they pick over every aspect of your business and decide whether to make you bankrupt or not.

- Trying to get supply from those creditors in the future and feeling like a naughty school boy or girl who has "learnt their lesson".

- Not being able to answer your phone because it might be somebody looking for money.

- Having holes in your shoes on wet days, having a car that breaks down.

- Not going to social functions because you can't afford to, and can't stand the looks of pity from your friends.

3. It's all about the money
– a little story

Okay what's the deal here? You promise "52 ways to make more money" and then you proceed to use up three of them preaching to me that **it is all about the money?** Well, yes – that's exactly what we're doing but look closely at the 52nd way and you'll notice we've dropped an extra "tip" in for you. So remain calm and let us carry on. We can't say this enough – **it's about the money.** You need to get that and then get it again. It's time for a true story.

Johnnie – true story

When I was young, naive and full of my own immortality, I had a very successful sandwich and coffee shop chain which was expanding at a ferocious rate. We were growing far too fast and although the business was basically profitable we had totally run out of cash. One of my business partners also acted as the accountant and unknown to me and my other partner had accrued huge debts in his own name.

One day we arrived into work to discover he had gone personally bankrupt and there were several huge "holes" in our accounts. Since it was a partnership, our bank financing immediately stopped and the wonderful growing business very quickly turned into a horrible, scary nightmare. We immediately removed the bankrupt partner and ran around like headless chickens pulling in cash from whatever source we could. Desperate to find a way to prop up the business and pay our suppliers while we tried to refinance.

A large customer put us in touch with a gentleman in his seventies who had previously helped him in a similar situation. This character was worth well in excess of £40 million and certainly had the financial wherewithal to rescue us. He arrived at the door in his huge Mercedes S500 but didn't cut much of a physical presence himself. He was small, wore a cheap brown suit and chain smoked the entire time he was with us.

"Okay boys – let's see where we are. How much money did you make last week?"

"Well", I spluttered, "we don't know that. We haven't even got our accounts for last year yet. How can we work out our profit for a week? There are four shops and a factory!"

"What do you mean you can't work out your profit for a week?" he asked with curious look on his face. "I have a big café over in Bangor and this is what I do ..."

He took out an old brown envelope from his pocket and with the cigarette hanging from his mouth started writing at the top of the page with a chewed Bic biro. "At the start of the week I count all the stock in the shop. Everything. Every single thing. Every tea bag, every sugar cube and every single item of food. And then do you know what I do?"

I glanced in a bemused fashion at my partner. "Errr. No."

"I record what I buy every day and record my sales every day. At the end of the week I count up all my wages and recount the stock. So what do you think I have then?"

Like a naïve fool, with my fancy business studies degree, I answered "errmmmmm, ehhhh …'

"I have my profit. I just take off the rent and a few other things and I have my profit. Every week. Every single week. I count at the start, count at the end and record during the week. Now, is that hard?"

"No, well, I suppose not. But what about depreciation and accruals?" I asked trying to pretend that I grasped the whole thing and was at least as clever as he was.

"Forget 'em. They don't matter for this. I can include them afterwards. These are your fundamentals. These businesses are simple but you gotta know your fundamentals. This is how it works. You pay X for your food, Y for your wages and what's left is your profit contribution. Do that and we'll know where you are. Now will you do that for me?"

"Okay," I mumbled. But I knew we wouldn't, and I think he knew we wouldn't too. We could never do that over all our shops and the factory. It would take up too much time and anyway you couldn't accurately tell how much money a business of our size was making with that method. Or so I thought.

So up he got, handed me the brown envelope with his spidery writing on it and jumped into his Mercedes. One week later he returned and asked for the figures. We mumbled and stuttered and made our excuses about being too busy trying to save the business. He fixed us with a cold stare, wished us good luck and left. I never saw him again.

Two weeks later we shut the doors on the business. We were unable to meet our creditors and had to lay off all thirty staff who worked in the factory. We sold the shops for a fraction of their true value and got together just enough money to stop us from going bankrupt.

A harsh lesson. Particularly harsh since we subsequently realised that since we had got rid of the accountant partner we had been making about £8000 profit a month. We could easily have saved the business with a relatively small cash injection and our friend with his sound fundamentals could have provided the money at the drop of a hat.

Fundamentals, fundamentals, fundamentals.

And the biggest fundamental of all is that **it's all about the money**. It's not about awards, it's not about ego, it's not even about seeing a customer's face when they've had a great cup of coffee or a wonderful lunch. It's about the money. It's about making really, really sure that the whole thing adds up. That you're not living in some romantic dream world of serving customers and keeping them happy and making sure they don't feel ripped off!

Needless to say, in any business that we have jointly or separately operated since then, the fundamentals are never ignored and we always, always, always do a weekly profit and loss. Always. The fundamentals of business are ultimately the same as the fundamentals of anything. If you don't get them right then you're sunk. So – is it clear? **It's all about the money.** Now let's move on…

4. Focus on coffee for profit

If it's **all about the money** then coffee is the key thing to focus on. It's easy to forget that the margin in coffee is so great. We often tend to look at total spend and the revenues from larger spend items such as lunch, whilst forgetting that the gross profit from two cups of premium coffee can easily be the same as a full meal. And it will have less of a labour cost attributed to it.

Too often coffee is an afterthought, a means to an end, and we either buy the cheapest brand available or are seduced by a hyped-up sales pitch. Operators rarely invest any time or money into researching, sourcing and purchasing the best coffees available. But they should, as the rewards are huge.

Coffee is not only a great margin product, it is a product, probably the only one on your menu, that customers will come back for several times during the week. But they will only come if you **"hook and addict"** them with a brilliant product. A coffee so compelling that they can't leave without a second cup. Or won't have lunch without a cup afterwards. Or sit at their desk in work thinking about how they can get a cup of your coffee to "keep them going".

Wake up to that great coffee taste

"If you do build a great experience, customers tell each other about that. Word of mouth is very powerful."

Jeff Bezos

Hugo – true story

I was sitting with a customer recently who operates a highly successful gastropub. They do great food and sell a huge range of speciality beers by draft. We decided to have our meeting off site and visited a local coffee shop. During the course of our meeting we had two cups of coffee each.

At the end of the meeting he remarked to me "how do these places make money? We've been sitting here for two hours and they've only had a few quid from us." His perspective was that in the bar the volume of money going through the till was so much higher. So I sat him back down and we analysed the facts.

The facts were that at that time of day (mid-afternoon) his bar was practically empty and the coffee shop was more than half full. As we dug deeper we discovered that the gross profit margin on our two coffees was exactly the same as it would be if we had bought two pints each in his bar. He may have had more money in his till but the cost of the beer was much higher. Slowly it dawned on him.

Don't be fooled by money in the till – money in the bank at the end of the month is all that matters. There's an old but valuable cliché that is worth trotting out:

"Turnover is vanity – profit is sanity."

5. Great coffee (profits) come from great training

There is great profit in coffee but you must be prepared to spend a little of that margin on training to make sure the product is good enough. Cheap machines, cheap coffee

Wake up to the value of training...
"What's going on in the inside shows on the outside."
Earl Nightingale

and poor training is simply a rip off. The customer knows it and they won't be back. These days people know what tastes great and what doesn't and you can't get away with a pot of stewed coffee any more if you want a lasting business.

As ever this comes down to a mindset. Often we simply don't treat coffee like a fine food that needs to be lovingly and skilfully prepared. **The margin is even greater than with our food** and yet we trust the preparation to untrained waiting staff in a way we would never trust food preparation.

This mindset from the top down needs to change. The staff need to fully understand that they are dealing with a sensitive product and that with a bit of care they can produce something really wonderful. The great thing is that this is actually remarkably easy. Staff generally love the theatre attached to coffee and enjoy being associated with the barista culture.

The secret to great coffee training (and profits) is to implement a good barista training programme.

This is an on-going commitment, particularly with the high staff churn in the industry. **Businesses that focus on the training are the ones that will make money at the coffee business.** Don't let anybody near coffee until they are at basic barista standard and challenge them to get to professional barista status by entering the World Barista Championship every year. The competition is run in most countries and will prove to be a strong and exciting motivator for your staff.

6. Great coffee sales come from one thing–great taste

Coffee Taste and The Coffee Experience move with consumer times, and yet they are timeless. Uncompromised taste will never go out of fashion and will always sell more coffee. You simply cannot expect to make money in the coffee business unless great tasting coffee is a major priority for you and all your employees. Consistent coffee comes from consistently and relentlessly controlling the brewing factors.

Freshness Wake Up Questions

■ When was your coffee brewed?

■ When was your coffee ground?

■ When was your coffee roasted?

Cleanliness Wake Up Questions

■ How dirty does your equipment look right now?

■ How clean is your water?

■ When was the last time you cleaned the screens/filters or pistons?

Extraction Wake Up Questions

■ Espresso - is your extraction time between 20 & 30 seconds?

■ Filter – have you tried golden cup standards - 90g to 3 pints?

■ Plunger – have you infused for 4 minutes?

These wake up calls are just for starters. We haven't even started on varietals, origins, roasting degrees and milk preparation techniques, so you need to do some pretty heavy research into the world of a cup of coffee and how to control enough factors to ensure that essential consistency. Coffee is at the heart of your business. **Treat it with serious respect**. Find a good advisor/supplier and get them to teach you how to buy coffee.

Wake up to expecting your coffee to taste excellent every time...

"High achievement always takes place in the framework of high expectation."

Charles F Kettering

Take care not to fall into the coffee marketers and salesmens trap. Clearly Sustainable Fairtrade, Organic, Bird Friendly, Shade, Rainforest Alliance, Utz Kapeh and other good coffee stories can be good for your business and good for others, but they are applicable only if you understand them first, can use them as part of your business plan and don't let them affect your taste standards. (You have a standard written down don't you?) The good coffee businesses need to be environmentally, socially **and** economically profitable.

Once you have established this great taste, you need to keep on top of it. You need it to be there in your induction programme. It needs to be there in your training and you need to keep checking. You need a formalised mystery shopper system in place and you must ask your regulars for constant feedback.

7. It's all about the food

Now that we have hopefully drummed into you the importance of the "money" you need to flip things round and see the whole enterprise from your customer's perspective. You must never forget about the money, but

Wake up to the power of great food and coffee...
"You do not merely want to be considered just the best of the best. You want to be considered the only one who does what you do."
Jerry Garcia

remember that all they care about is the value you're going to give them for **their hard-earned money**. And that means you have to provide great food. Great food creates a happy customer who gives you more money. Simple as that? Well not quite, but read on.

We all know a few businesses that seem to survive sometimes surprisingly long periods of time serving bad food. They are rare though, and are generally situated in odd locations where the competition is minimal.

Over the years between us we have owned or worked with a huge variety of food businesses. The one thing that marks out the most successful operations is great food. Good food doesn't have to be expensive or fancy – one of our best businesses was a Fish and Chip shop for example – but it does have to be as appetizing and tasty as you can possibly make it.

If you're going to produce something simple like a ham sandwich ensure it's as good a ham sandwich as you can possibly make. Make sure you'd feel comfortable serving it to your family for a big occasion. Make it so you'd serve it to a potential future spouse after a first date.

Make your muffins, scones or biscuits or whatever you are serving, as good or great as you possibly can. Slave over the recipes and sit up late at night in your own kitchen experimenting. If you don't cook yourself then drum into your kitchen staff or suppliers that you simply can't and won't accept anything other than wonderful food.

There are dozens of café options for your customers to choose from and it's up to you to create some part of your offer that really appeals to them and keeps them coming back. You need to have a hook or variety of hooks on your menu that will keep them coming back day after day.

In the past we, or our clients, have created a variety of excellent products that are appreciably different from competitors' products and can be justifiably loudly and proudly promoted. Apple and cinnamon scones, the world's best Croque Monsieur, cherry brownies, huge apple pies, superfood flapjacks. The list is endless but **your shop needs a few "stars"** that can appeal at every time of the day. You need a product that jumps out of the menu, is delicious and (relatively) unique, and can be eaten morning, lunch and afternoon helping to keep all parts of the day as busy as possible.

This doesn't mean that the rest of the items on your menu should be mediocre. Everything should be delicious, but you must have a few "halo" products. Products that you can shout about and use to show your customers the level of effort and care that you put into your food. This helps to provide confidence in the rest of your offer and enables your business to stand out from the crowd.

Hugo – true story

Many years ago I had a friend who decided to open a chain of cafés. He had come from a manufacturing background and felt that the coffee business was an easy way to make money. He had big plans, a big budget, and he was going to roll them out and make his millions.

He insisted, no matter how strongly I tried to persuade him otherwise, that all the food could simply come in the back door from the cheapest supplier and that the coffee should be capable of being made by a monkey. Ideally he wanted a machine that could simply produce money. He wanted a "production line" version of a coffee shop.

He set up his café and sourced a variety of products. He put in great systems and even created a reasonable looking business.

But he forgot the key missing ingredient. He forgot "passion". The business was utterly soulless. He had no passion in his coffee and none in his food. Great passion creates great tasting food and coffee. There was nothing that the staff could rave about and nothing that could "hook and addict" the customers to return.

It failed. Quickly and painfully. And, like so many others before him, he chose to blame the location and the economy.
Slowly it dawned on him.

8. There are three ways and only three ways to grow your business

An American marketing guru by the name of Jay Abraham popularised this concept and it's a great way to view your business. Hopefully it will be a proper **"light bulb" moment** for you, just as it was for us. Abraham says that you can only grow your business three ways:

1. By increasing the number of customers you have.
2. By increasing the number of times those customers visit you or give you money in any form.
3. By increasing the amount of money those customers give you.

The great thing about this concept is the way it dramatically increases your profits if you can systematically concentrate on all three. Increase the number of customers you have by 10% and your sales will rise by 10%. Increase all three by 10% and the way the maths works your overall sales will increase by 33%. Increase all three by 100% and your overall sales will rise by 800%.

Don't worry about the maths – just accept that it is true then sit down and take all three parts of your business and systematically work on them. Getting new customers is actually the hardest and most expensive thing to do, so concentrate on the other two first and then generate a little extra revenue which can be put towards getting new customers.

Increasing customer spend by 10% can be as simple as raising prices. But raising prices coupled with changing the way staff communicate to them, offering larger sized coffees, selling more food items with their coffee, second cups of coffee and so on could very quickly see a much larger increase.

Getting your customers to visit more often can be achieved in a variety of different ways. Converting that three visit a week customer to four visits a week can be attained simply by making the quality of your coffee so good that he can't pass by your shop without nipping in. Alternatively, you can try and persuade your morning customers to try you for lunch or your afternoon customers to try you in the morning. Maybe you can persuade your weekday customers to visit at the weekend or all of your customers to take food home or use you for catering functions. Whatever you decide to do, the "Three Ways" rule gives you an excellent basis on which to plan and **grow your business**.

Wake up to trying out new ideas

"I don't understand why people are frightened of new ideas. I'm frightened of the old ones."

John Cage

9. Be brave with your prices

Nothing hurts your ability to make profit from your coffee business more than being cowardly with your prices. Far too many operators are scared of offending customers by charging properly for their food and coffee. **You must be proud of your product and charge accordingly**. Fighting for business on price is the surest way to go out of business. You must charge enough and have a simple enough menu system so that you don't delay increasing prices due to the cost of implementing any changes.

The best solution is to be at the upper end of the pricing scale from your competitors and to increase prices little and often to avoid any big shock rises. Price increases always need to be accompanied with a little bit of staff training to ensure the right message is given to your customers. They need to understand how hard it is to make a profit and how expensive it is to keep the business going. You do not want employees to be telling customers that you have just bought a new car and need to pay for it! Increases in rent, rates, water charges and taxes are all reasonable and highly valid excuses. Increase in minimum wage is a trickier one, even though it is generally relevant, simply because it invites negative comment from the employee who is telling the customer why the cost of their coffee has increased.

Wake up to listening to everybody at the expense of your intuition

"Problems cannot be solved by the same level of thinking that created them."
Albert Einstein

Johnnie – true story

Running a successful café a few years ago we had a complex menu system that was expensive to change as it required the services of a signwriter. That, coupled with too many people involved in the decision making process, meant that we didn't increase prices for two years. Far, far too long a period of time in a coffee shop.

Finally I bit the bullet and increased the prices by a fairly blanket 10% across the board. We had a total of three comments from customers only one of which was a complaint. The rest barely noticed.

At the end of the first week I broke down the weekly till readings and analysed them. We turned over a total of £9,567 after VAT. Under the old prices this would have been £8,187. Since there was no increase in overhead (other than the minimal sign writing cost) this meant that we had put a total of £1,410 to the bottom line. More than £70,000 extra profit simply for being brave.

Just how much money had we left on the table in the previous year by not increasing prices? Make sure you don't make the same mistake.

10. Know your figures and have a plan–a plan that works for you!

What do you want from the business? You need to establish exactly what you want from it in terms of the hours you wish to work and the sort of revenue you need or want it to generate.

You have to know your own figures and know what you want to do with them. At the start of every year (either financial or calendar) you must sit down and decide what it is that you want to do with your business for that year. Take your previous year's accounts and set some difficult but achievable goals based on them. You know what you were slack at during the past year – make sure that doesn't happen again and develop a clear plan to see these "resolutions" through.

Wake up to why you might have no profit...
"We tend to get what we expect."
Norman Vincent Peale

If your gross margin was sitting at 70% the previous year then make a target of 73% and produce a written plan for how you're going to achieve this. Better buying, price increases, more effective food costing and pricing, less wastage or making better coffee. However you're going to do it, get it down on paper and attach a deadline to the plan.

You need to take all the financial aspects of the business and have a target for them. Don't go through the year rudderless just "expecting" to make more money. It won't happen.

Wake up to allocating the right resource to your coffee production...
"Time is our most valuable asset, yet we tend to waste it, kill it, and spend it rather than invest it."
Jim Rohn

But make sure it's not just about the financial side of the business. If you are working a 60 hour week and never seeing your family then the business simply isn't working for you. It is a dangerous myth that hospitality businesses require huge hours from the owners and you need to make sure that you don't fall into that trap. If you're working too hard then employ better staff and train them to do some of your job. **Put in systems** to ensure the business runs just as well when you're not there as it does when you are.

11. Get accountable and know your figures

The key to making profit in your coffee business is to know your numbers and ensure you have clear and simple procedures to track them. Daily, weekly and monthly – NOT once a year six months after your financial year end when your accountant finally bothers to get round to looking at your books.

The numbers don't lie in any aspect of your life. If your doctor has told you to take better care of yourself he's going to measure some numbers. He's going to take your weight, your heart rate, your blood pressure and a cholesterol reading. When you go back in six months and you haven't done anything but eat cake the numbers won't lie. They'll tell him the story.

It's the same thing with your business. If it's out of shape then you have to take those numbers and keep measuring them. You need to realistically work out where you are and then create a plan that alters those numbers in the right direction. Don't live in a dream world of denial and metaphorically sit eating cake to make yourself feel happy.

> ### *Wake up to the facts*
> *"If knowledge can create problems,
> it is not through ignorance that we
> can solve them."*
> Isaac Asimov

12. Know your food cost for every single item

In the food and coffee business your food cost is one of the two key numbers that you must have total control over. You need to know your food cost every week. Every single week. You have got to know how much it costs you to create the level of sales you achieved. Count your stock at the beginning of the week and at the end of the week and then sit down and count your invoices. **The numbers won't lie.**

Control waste and develop systems to check wastage levels. Create simple wastage sheets and most importantly make sure they are filled in with a monetary value. Consider using clear bin bags so that everyone is more aware of what is being thrown out. Make sure every item has a PLU key on the till. Compare theory with actual every week. Get this – 2% variance on a £300K café is £6k off the bottom line.

Consider bin bag audits to ensure that proper procedures are being adhered to. It isn't fun but it makes it very easy to check up on how well the kitchen is being run and how tight things are. Worried that you might be offending staff? May we refer you to **Number One?**

Knowing your food costs for each item and having a clear understanding of how the margins differ between products will help to fuel your marketing. The reason we love coffee so much is because the margin is so great. But don't forget that a lower percentage margin can still mean a higher pound note margin. In other words, a bundled lunch deal with an overall margin of 60% may profit more physical gross profit in the till than a lower spend at 75%.

Percentage margins are important – but only as a tool. What really matters are the pounds and the pence you have left at the end of the week that belong to you. You can't deposit percentages in the bank.

Wake up to using your information carefully

"Knowledge is power"
Sir Francis Bacon

13. Know your labour/wage cost and stay accountable

The second key number to control is your wage cost. This is an exercise which needs to be done daily – not something that you chance upon at the end of the year or even the month. You need a realistic view daily and weekly.

Many operators live in a dream world where they simply won't take full account of the **real cost of employees**. They look at the hourly wage and take that as the true cost. You need to factor in employee national insurance and holidays. That's more than 20% before you even get started or consider sick pay and other issues. Be utterly, utterly realistic about this and do not allow yourself to be fooled.

Watch clock-in procedures like a hawk and be very aggressive about malpractice. They must clock themselves in. Make it a dismissible offence in your contract to disobey this rule. Any clock-in errors must be dealt with immediately and clearly.

Make sure they know that there is always something to be done. Standing around doing nothing is not acceptable. If it's quiet you should consider training floor staff to do a bit of kitchen prep or some deep cleaning. Always have a list with "things to do when it's quiet" available so that there is no excuse.

And if you are overstaffed don't be embarrassed to ask some of your employees if they want to go home. You can't force them (in most situations) but you may find that some of them have other things they need to get done at home.

14. It's your fault–get this and then get it again

This is the most crucial concept of business ownership or management. Get this, really get it, and things start to become easier. If you don't get it then you are doomed to a life of mediocrity and bitterness. A life of always blaming the economy or your boss/wife/parents/kids/landlord – the list is endless. You'll lie in your old people's home, with your incontinence pants on, muttering and moaning and complaining to anyone who'll listen, but they'll all be avoiding you!

So here it is – the key to business success:
"Anything and everything that happens in your business is your fault."

If you decide you're big enough and ugly enough to have a business then decide that you will take full responsibility for it. Don't blame the competition, interest rates, the economy, your staff or anything else. Accept that it's **your** business or that **you** have been given the responsibility to run it by the owner. If you want the rewards from a successful business then you have to accept that, on occasion, challenges will arise and it won't all be plain sailing.

But if you acknowledge that a problem is your fault and therefore your responsibility, then you can calmly accept it and try and come up with the solution. Success in business is NEVER a straight line. It is always a wiggly line that sometimes moves backwards. Just accept this and don't beat yourself up over the problems that will arise but do deal with them. As fast, efficiently and quickly as possible.

Hugo – true story

In our coffee distribution business we have a great reputation for delivering a quality "total solution" product that includes coffee, equipment, training, marketing and quality auditing. One day I was asked by a significant volume customer to supply his group exclusively with a quality coffee only as he had his own brewing equipment. This appeared attractive in volume terms but I knew it was going to be very difficult to control the brewing factors and therefore the 'in the cup' taste quality. We discussed what was required by both of us for several days.

After careful consideration I said no to his request because I knew that he was going to use his new coffee to relaunch his business and that we were never going to be able to get them to take enough responsibility for making great coffee. A competitor got the business and he launched a new coffee offer, but it was just not good or consistent enough. The business was eventually sold to one of my customers and we gained credibility because we had said no to the original proposal. It's important to learn exactly what your market is and not try to be all things to all people. Occasionally saying no is a crucial part of that.

15. A coffee shop is all about people–and people need clear rules

Make sure you understand this. It is not a production line with impressive machinery. It's about kitchen staff working with counter staff dealing with the public. **Get your rules together and stick to them**. Make your employees grasp that the business is an extension of you. But do not, under any circumstances, play the game of "being the boss" or arrogantly strut around the place because you're the "owner."

If you are working daily on the site and your employees have to pay for their lunch and are only allowed a sandwich, then so are you. If they aren't allowed a premium coffee for their break, then neither are you. Play the game. If you bend the rules for yourself then you bend the rules for them.

The rules are slightly different if you have several sites but still need to be kept very clear. When you eat in a site and don't pay you need to make sure it is clearly recorded so that you don't let any control slip.

If they see you eating free food or "entertaining" a friend or family member, that could be a green light for them to steal and justify the reduced margin by saying that the boss is eating the profits.

Owning a coffee business is **about the money** – it's not about the perks of free food or the ego of being an "owner".

Have you ever had a boss or teacher who would say to you "do as I say but not as I do"? Remember just how annoying and frustrating that was? Well, put yourself in your employees' shoes and always make sure your philosophy is "do as I do".

Johnnie – true story

Many years ago I had an opportunity to go into business with a wealthy friend who had money and wanted to diversify. He had a successful food distribution business and felt that owning a good coffee shop would help him present a certain image to his clients.

We went a fair way down the road of looking at sites until I had an enlightening conversation with him about how to manage staff. His solution was to "shout at them until they get the message".

He also explained how impressive he felt it would be to sit and have his meetings in the café and not pay for the food because he "owned" it. Slowly and quietly he dropped the whole idea. This is an utterly infuriating situation for employees and is always doomed to failure. It may work if you are Peter Stringfellow stuck in the corner of your nightclub but in the general coffee business it is irritating for employees and confusing for customers.

16. Make sure your employees understand the numbers

Never underestimate just how naive your employees are about the concept of profit. **They will always overestimate your profit** and underestimate just how hard it is to make money in this business. The minute you get busy at any level they will spend hours discussing with their friends and co-workers just what a "gold-mine" your coffee shop must be and just how little you pay them compared to what you must be making.

You need to change this perception and make very sure they know exactly how hard it is to make a profit. Use a simple food item such as a muffin and cut it up into the various pieces to illustrate where the money goes. Cut off 17.5% for the VAT or whatever your sales tax is to begin with. Then cut off the physical cost of the muffin. Now remove the wage cost adding in and explaining the cost of employer's national insurance, holiday pay and sick pay. Now remove chunks for rent, rates, electricity and all your other expenses.

Try, where possible, to include actual figures. There is absolutely no point in hiding the economics of running a business from them and there is great benefit to letting them know the gory details. Include costs for accountants, lawyers and various other professionals who you may have to deal with. If your electrical bills are £1000 a quarter then tell them this. Add in all those little extras that they forget you have to pay for until you end up with five to ten percent of your muffin left. If you lost money last year then remove it all. **It's an eye-opening session** which helps explain the concept of profit a heck of a lot more effectively than trying to show them a profit and loss sheet.

Johnnie – true story

I can clearly remember, at the age of 14, standing with my brother discussing just how much money the owner of the ice cream café we worked in must be making. We reckoned he must be making about a 70% net profit. Youthful naivety? Perhaps – but only a little. I once asked the same question to more than thirty mature members of staff who worked for me in our sandwich bars. On average they reckoned we were keeping nearly 50% of the cost of each sandwich sold.

17. Every pound is not equal. A pound earned is worth a lot less than a pound saved

Getting new customers and creating extra sales is the exciting and sexy part of running a business but if ultimately you just want to make more money (and you do – don't you? See **Number One**) then you need to look at saving costs.

A pound earned needs to have the physical cost of the food or drink removed. It also requires input from a paid employee to produce it. Ultimately a pound earned is little more than ten or twenty pence (if you're lucky) in your back pocket.

But a pound saved is a full pound in your back pocket. A spoon, costing a pound that is saved from the bin is a full pound you will have left at the end of the year. Keep this in mind – and in the mind of your staff. Make sure you devote at least as much time to keeping costs down as you do to driving new customers through the door or selling more to your existing ones.

18. View your coffee business as though you were a customer

Walk and think, walk and think. Make sure you regiment this into every member of staff. The reality is that we all very quickly lose sight of the fact that a customer sees things very differently to the managers and employees. What you and your staff think is important is not necessarily important to your customers.

A new customer will be intimidated 90% of the time. We are all slightly awkward in a new environment, so view your business from a new customer's eyes as much as from an existing customer's. It's a fine balance. You need to grasp that the new customer will be confused about how you operate so you need to make your systems as clear as possible without being clumsy. Is it table service or counter service? Where do I get a tray? Where do I pay? If there is the slightest doubt about these things then make it very clear to them.

Consider getting staff to ask customers whether they have been at your café before. If they haven't then get the staff member to politely explain how you operate - where to order, where and when to pay and which products the server particularly likes themselves. Create a training session where staff role play at being a new customer, and make them understand that the script can be amended into their own words (within reason).

Existing customers need to see regular changes and new offers to keep them interested. But don't forget that your core menu items must be there every day. No excuses. Your customers have routines and if you're really, really lucky you can become part of their daily routine. Make sure that what they expect is there every day – come hell or high water.

Hugo – true story

For a long time we have known that coffee needs to taste great which is why we put so much emphasis on training. When we also made sure that the presentation was good (we taste with our eyes) it further increased sales. We took this further with several key customers using smell and noted that if we appealed to more than two senses at the same time we could, in many cases, double sales. In one particular case we modelled one of our favourite pub customers who always talked about how important music was and how it could significantly change the mood. We took advice and put together a very particular jazz track list and found that more than a third of the completed comment cards mentioned the fantastic music.

It is remarkable how strongly music can impact on the experience. If the customer likes the appearance of their cup of coffee, loves the taste and is comfortable with the ambience then they'll be happy. And happier customers spend more money!

Johnnie – true story

When I ran my first café/sandwich bar I made sure, by working like a maniac, that every day – every single day, we had every item on the menu. When we expanded our enterprise I would slowly see that some of the shops didn't have the full menu available. Why not? It was simple for me so why couldn't it be simple for the manager of that particular shop? It all came down to systems. Get the systems right, but make sure they are focused on what the customer wants and what the customer expects.

Walk your business several times daily with your "customer eyes" on. Walk it at opening, mid-morning, pre-lunch, mid-lunch, post lunch and mid-afternoon. Customer eyes. Get all staff to think this way.

19. View the business every day as if you were an employee

Think about working in your business from your employees' perspective. Just because you may not actually be working there doesn't mean that the standards need to slip in terms of facilities.

In the same way that you have to force yourself to see the café as a customer, force yourself to see it as a front line employee. If you create a decent environment for your staff you'll hold onto them much, much longer. Simple as that. And if you hold onto the good ones longer, you'll make more money. The costs of employing new staff are high. New employees need training and will make more mistakes with the customers which will cost you sales or may even result in the loss of a good customer that you've worked so hard to get.

So keep 'em happy. It makes sense – and money. But only to a point. Make it crystal clear at interview, induction and ongoing training that this it is a working environment. That you expect work from them. That if they work for you they have made a **commitment to work** – not a commitment to having fun in a holiday camp.

20. Break the whole selling process down and make it better

Be your own auditor. And not a stuffy, overpaid financial auditor who looks at your books every year and tries to find out if you've been helping yourself to a little "cash", or suspects you of boasting to your friends about what a great wee business you have, patting your back pocket in the process.

Nope – we mean a business auditor. Someone who applies the same level of detail as your accountant, but also scrutinises all the other operational aspects of your business. Do it slowly and methodically but start with the customer buying process. Look at all the aspects of how a customer might view your shop when they first come in. What will they see, is it inviting, are you upselling them, showing them something interesting? Are your menus clear, is your stock well displayed, is it logically displayed? What do your staff say? How efficiently are they charged? **Look at the whole process** and try to make every single stage just a little bit better for you, the customer and your staff.

Get employees involved. Ask your regular customers what frustrates them. Watch and observe to see where any delays or glitches occur. What you're trying to do is find out what parts of the business just aren't working properly. Maybe it's customer flow, maybe your till system is clumsy and slow, maybe your kitchen design is all wrong and creates too much work. Maybe you have too many people doing the ordering and no system to show what has been ordered if one person falls sick.

Whatever the problems are, find them and fix them.

21. Keep your toilets spotless

Why? Surely that won't make you money? Wrong. It's almost the easiest way to make more money, since the link between the cleanliness in your toilets and the cleanliness of your kitchen is very strong in your customer's mind.

I know a couple who have two main criteria when they visit a restaurant or coffee shop. Is the food "piping" hot and **are the toilets spotless?** They could be served muck or treated with indifference by the staff, but if the food is really hot and you could eat off the toilet seat then they'll be loyal forever.

Obviously that's an extreme example, but don't dismiss it too quickly. It is enormously off-putting to people on a conscious and subconscious level to visit dirty toilets. Keep them spotlessly clean, checked and signed at least every hour (ideally every half hour) and, after a trip to your loo, your customers will feel comfortable enough to sit back down and maybe have that second cup of coffee after all.

22. Treat lunch like a restaurant

Coffee signals the end of the meal, so make it easy for your customers to get coffee afterwards and buy a soft drink during their meal.

Many coffee shop owners don't take proper advantage of their lunch time business. A well run restaurant will attempt to sell you as much as possible during this period in as subtle a way as possible. They will offer drinks before food, wine with food and ideally sell you a starter, main course and dessert coupled with a side dish or two. And they will always sell you coffee at the end of the meal.

Most coffee bars & cafes will have a different format, but make sure you aren't leaving money on the table that the customer should ideally be spending with you and not somewhere else. At the very least you want to be **selling them two drinks** – a cold drink during the lunch and a coffee afterwards. Make sure you have the systems in place to do this easily. If you have table service, ensure your staff are adequately trained to offer this, and with counter service make it easy for the customer to get back to the till to get a coffee afterwards and not be put off by the continuing daunting queue. As ever, never forget the margin available in the coffee sales. And obviously coffee with dessert is a much better sale than coffee on its own.

Again, harping back to **points one, two and three – it's about the money**. But it's also about the customer's enjoyment. Lunch with a delicious dessert and an excellent cup of coffee is simply a better lunch. It's a better experience. You mustn't bully them into buying more, but make sure you have done everything in your power to offer them coffee and dessert and let them make the decision themselves. Too often coffee shop owners believe they are doing the customer a favour by not trying to sell them other items. It simply isn't the case.

23. Create food stories about your star products and sell, sell, sell

We're willing to bet that you have plenty of stories about some of your products. The star products that we discussed in **number seven** perhaps will all have some sort of story to them. Isn't there an old family recipe somewhere in your lunchtime mix, or maybe a cake recipe from your grandmother? Make a story about these items, tell the customers how they ended up on your menu, and shout about how proud you are of them. Even if the recipe was relatively simply put together by yourself, you can **create a story** to make it seem more interesting.

Don't forget that most regular customers are actually fascinated by the whole process of running a coffee business. Many of them sit there in their tedious little day jobs dreaming about the day they get made redundant or win the lottery and can finally own their own little slice of heaven – a coffee business.

We all know that this is a long way from reality, but play this fantasy up in your stories. The notion of you sitting with your chef dreaming up delicious new sweet things for your customers to eat, or finding an old recipe in a dust covered book in your grandmother's attic, is enormously compelling to many people. Maybe you had to bribe the owner of a café in Italy to give you a recipe for his buns. Or maybe you had to buy a couple of cakes and take them to a local baker to have them analysed because the café owner wouldn't, under any circumstances, give you the recipe.

Perhaps you buy cinnamon for your buns from a certain part of Sri Lanka because you noticed it tasted much better than all the rest. Or possibly your coffee comes from a particular estate or region (think wine) or is part of the 'Cup of Excellence' programme – the next big thing in coffee.

The messages you create need to be coherent and clear though. You're trying to make your customers think that you go to the ends of the earth to provide the best food and coffee just for them. You're subtly trying to emphasise that you use expensive ingredients and therefore must charge a little more. You're trying to get them to understand that **you really care about the food you serve**. Within your stories you need to have all those messages subtly hidden.

The stories you create must be clearly articulated to your staff and also clearly, but relatively discreetly, applied to table talkers, product labels and posters. Staff and customers alike must buy into the concept and believe the stories, so each one needs to be as truthful as possible. Don't run the risk of a fantastical story being questioned by a customer and one of your staff saying "oh, he just made that up – we buy them in Tesco." You must have integrity in your business, as blatant lies will be seen through very quickly.

Combine your stories with BOGOF offers and distribute them to your mailing list, through a leaflet drop or in an advertisement in your local paper.

Johnnie – true story

One of the biggest lessons I ever learnt about food marketing involved a fish and chip shop I owned a few years ago. We worked extremely hard to create perfect chips and every item on our menu was meticulously sourced to ensure we had the best fish and chips for miles around. We tried, for example, twenty three different oil and dripping combinations and brands to ensure we had chips that were absolutely perfect. The site was in an odd location however, and although we were making profit, we weren't making very much.

I discovered that, far from being bored with my stories about just how much effort we had put in to making every item on the menu, friends and family were genuinely interested. I decided to write down the story of each item and took out six consecutive weekly quarter page advertisements in the local paper. The ads looked like newspaper articles with one small product photograph and relayed my story in great detail.

At the bottom of each advertisement was a simple "Buy One Get One Free" voucher.

These advertisements literally transformed the business and very quickly our weekly products were tripled. Of course not everybody read every word of each long advertisement, but they did read enough to know that we really cared about our food and really had gone to a lot of effort.

We have subsequently used that technique to great effect in many coffee businesses highlighting amongst other things - apple pies, scones, coffee cake and biscuits.

Hugh has been very successful with numerous customers using this technique and indeed it was the basis of his first ever Coffee Profit Presentation in 2000 at The Speciality Coffee Association Annual Conference in America.

24. Get crafty with your menu and signage

After you have been through your food costing process you'll discover you have a number of high margin items on the menu. As long as you can stand over these items as being excellent you need to **push them just a little bit harder** than the low margin alternatives. A good example of this is the difference between a properly made brownie and a scone. The brownie could cost three times more to make and you're unlikely to have a price premium of more than 50%. So this gives you an opportunity to push the scones and make them part of your "story".

At its most simple you can just highlight these various items in red on your menu. Or pick them out in bold or with a slightly larger font. You don't need to explain why you're picking them out since the customer will automatically assume that they are "special" and will be more tempted to try them.

Another alternative is to highlight these items on table talkers or little A5 card holders beside where you merchandise your product. "Have you tried our……?" is an enormously effective way of drawing attention to whatever item it is that you are promoting.

Beware of treating high percentage margin items as the Holy Grail though. At the end of the day **it's all about money** and your goal should be to achieve as high a pound note margin per customer as possible and not just a high percentage margin.

In other words, if you can achieve a higher pound note profit from your brownie then don't push the scone to the exclusion of this item. It's all about knowing your margins and food costs like it was

Wake up to thinking differently

"It is not worth an intelligent man's time to be in the majority. By definition, there are already enough people to do that."

G. H. Hardy

second nature. You need to reach a stage where you instantly know the cost of every item on your menu without even thinking about it.

25. Watch your language

You need to make sure that all employees are speaking the way you want them too. This can be tough because you don't want them to appear to be selling too strongly and you clearly don't want the kind of scripted brain dead nonsense that we have to endure from the burger chains. When people visit your business they won't, either subconsciously or consciously, tolerate staff like that and ultimately it will harm your business.

What you do need to do is make sure that they are **using the right expressions** for a number of key issues. Ideally you'll be running your business in such a ruthlessly efficient manner that you never sell out of anything, but if, on the rare occasion that you do, you certainly don't want an employee to tell the customer "we ran out". You need them to say something like: "sadly that was very popular today and I'm afraid it's all gone, but have you tried our…?" When asked about an item you don't want them to say "I don't like that", or "I don't know what it's like", or even "they're all nice". You need them to inject a bit of personality and encourage them to use their own preferences. "This is my favourite", "these are delicious", or "I love this one and it's really popular".

It's all about constantly enthusing about the quality of your product. You can't expect your employees to love everything, but you can expect them to enthusiastically sell those items they do like. If there is nothing they like on the menu then you either need to change that employee or rethink your menu. Food needs to be sold with passion.

26. Say hello

Just say it. Just bloody say it. "Hello". "Hi". "Good morning". "Good afternoon". It doesn't really matter but the first thing a customer should hear is "Hello" or ideally, if they are a regular, "Hello Mrs. Jones", and the first thing they should see is a smile.

Let us put it this way, you have two types of customer:

1. Existing customers who have been before and have already given you a fair bit of money. Surely they deserve a "hello" for their loyalty? Surely they deserve a smile and an acknowledgement of the fact that you value them coming through the door.

2. New customers who are trying you out for the first time. A pleasant "hello" and a smile are so rare these days that it marks you out as a good place to visit before they've even tried your coffee.

Worried that this is too cheesy? **Try it yourself**. Walk into a variety of shops or cafes and gauge how you feel when you are greeted with a smile and a "hello" versus the feelings you have when you are ignored. And most of all it costs nothing.

Wake up to your customer
"You can never tell what type of impact you may make on another's life by your actions or lack of action. Sometimes just a smile on the street to a passing stranger can make a difference we could never imagine."
Ed Foreman

Just, as Nike say, do it!

27. Don't point and watch your body language

Don't point to the table – it's rude. Instead gesture with an open palm. You may be aware of the old "78% of communication is non-verbal" line. The original study that came up with that theory is probably the most misquoted study in the history of human behaviour! But at its heart lies a strong basic truth – what we say is only part of the deal. How we say it and what we do while we are saying it is vitally important.

This is why the whole burger chain strategy, where a vacant looking teenager reads from a script to upsell us to large fries, is very often doomed to failure. Within the coffee business the customer has a very different expectation of how they expect to be spoken to. You must ensure your employees are using body language that means they actually care about what they're saying.

One of the simple rules that you can teach them is to avoid pointing – at anything – ever! **Always gesture with an open palm**. If the customer is asking where the toilet is, or which table to sit at, then make sure you open your palm and show them in a friendly manner. Do not point. Better still, walk them there (note the big supermarkets all do this…it's in their training programme!)

As ever, think about this yourself from a customer perspective. It's basic common sense, but we forget about it far too often in the day to day "efficient" running of our businesses. We hate to have people in shops pointing at us. It's just rude. And, as ever, if you make them feel comfortable and welcome they'll stay and maybe come back again. And if they stay then they'll hopefully buy another coffee and maybe you'll get that holiday to the Maldives after all!

28. Nod your head when asking a customer if they would like something

Woop – woop – sneaky tactic alert. Call the café police. This is a cracking wee tactic, but you do need to be careful of it. If you ask the customer would they like something to eat as well as their coffee and simply nod and smile at the same time, you will get an appreciably higher amount of sales. If you make the same offer and shake your head and frown you will get an appreciably lower amount of sales.

We have tested this in a pretty rigorous way in a number of environments and it **always makes a difference.** Just try it out and see. It's sneaky, but not so sneaky that you can actually change someone's mind. Research has shown that this technique can only reinforce what they are already thinking about. So if a customer wants something to eat but is trying to argue with themselves not to have it, then your wee nod can tip them over the edge. If they really don't want something because they've just eaten a huge lunch then you could be nodding like one of those stupid dogs in the back of a car and it won't make a blind bit of difference.

So get all worries of "mind control" out of your head and just try it out. It **will** make a difference. Trust us. We're lovely guys, really.

29. Thank them

It's obvious, but again chronically overlooked. We respond very positively to "Pleases" and "Thank-Yous" and these days basic politeness is sadly rare. Use this to your advantage – there is no need to be sycophantic but if a customer has come in and given you money then **thank them**. Simple as that. They had a choice and they chose you, so make an effort to thank them.

If you are the owner never underestimate the importance of making contact with your regulars too when they have company with them. The power of "knowing the owner" is a strange and powerful phenomenon. We all want others to think that we are important and popular and as the owner you can help make your customer feel a little better. Do the rounds, clear a few tables, and take time to say "hello, how are you" to as many even vaguely familiar faces as possible.

Don't forget, it's all about making your customers feel good and ensuring that they want to be in **your** coffee bar and not the shiny new one that has opened five doors down. Use as many of the free tricks in your armoury as possible.

Wake up to handling that nasty customer...

"Holding anger is like grasping a hot coal with the intent of throwing it at someone else; you are the one who gets burned."
The Buddha

30. The Granny Rule

Would you say it to your granny? That's the level of respect your customers need to be given. Look at every piece of communication within your business as if you were dealing with your granny as a customer. Of course if your granny happens to be like the wicked witch from Disney's Snow White, then you probably need to think of a kindly aunt instead. (If you can't think of any kindly old lady you knew as a child, you may have some personality issues. You should possibly go and work for the government in some tedious clerical job where you can complain all the time about the 52 days holiday you get a year.)

But generally we have a high level of reverence for our grannies. We treat them in a very respectful way because they usually mean so much to us. They gave us 50p when our parents weren't looking and allowed us to eat far more sweets and chocolate than was strictly wise. It's this respect that you need to apply to your customers. At the end of the day it isn't your granny who pays your mortgage and rent on your café (unless you're very lucky) but it's your customers who do. You should actually be treating them better than your granny.

Johnnie – true story

In my early days of business my granny used to regularly visit me and have a cup of coffee. A successful local businessman who used to occasionally offer me advice happened to be in the shop one day when she was there. I introduced her to him and we had a pleasant chat.

After she had gone he said to me:

"Right, now you know how to use the Granny Rule."

"Eh?" I replied, totally bemused.

"Treat every customer the same way you would treat your granny. I saw the level of respect you offered her and the obvious joy you felt at having her in your business. Deal with every customer that way and you can't fail."

"Brilliant", I said, truly getting the concept, "but what about my staff?"

He paused and looked at me like I wasn't exactly the brightest tool in the box. "Well, Mr. Fancy Degree boy, you just get them to assume the customer is their granny!"

So that's what I do. And every time I see a member of staff treating a customer with an element of disdain or even a slightly "off" tone I ask them, "Would you speak like that to your granny?"

It's a great and simple concept and incredibly powerful. I've yet to find a single employee who didn't immediately grasp it and deal with customers better as a result. Try it.

31. Keep the kids occupied

The happier the kids are the happier the parents will be. Also, if you keep them occupied you keep the other customers happy too. It's simple and cheap but requires just a little thought. Be flexible (within reason) with your portions for kids. Consider creating kid-specific products and make sure they are as healthy and as additive free as possible. That doesn't mean you have to give them a piece of broccoli – just make sure your buns are fat free, or whatever the current health fixation is. If you're going to provide crayons make sure they aren't ancient and filthy, and ensure you have plenty of paper and decent clean and safe toys for the babies to play with.

It's worth experimenting with colouring-in sheets that are tailored to your business. You could consider getting a local art student to create line drawings of your star products that then form the basis of the colouring-in book. You can also create **monthly or weekly competitions** that have a prize for various age groups. Puzzles or quizzes by age groups are always successful…they always want to do the older one! Consider very small prizes (lollipops, sweets etc.) for every entry.

What you're trying to achieve is a little pester-power from the child to the parent. If the child is happy and wants to be in your coffee bar then the parent will be happy too and feel comfortable enough to maybe buy another cup of coffee. Which, of course, is what it's all about.

But there is a proviso to this one. If you don't like children or maybe have a sophisticated food offer, then don't force yourself to be child friendly. As long as you accept that you will have a reduced market then stick to your convictions. We have a number of sophisticated clients who almost actively dissuade children. There are many little niches within the market and you mustn't feel you need to cover them all.

32. Sell more coffee with cake and more cake with coffee. Up-selling and cross-selling

We constantly meet clients who are uncomfortable with the whole cross-selling concept – i.e. selling a complementary product with their primary purchase. They feel that this is bullying the customer into buying something they don't really want. Usually this simply isn't the case. Very often the customer actually does want something to eat with their coffee, but you just haven't made it easy enough to tip them over into a purchase.

Whether a customer is on a diet or not simply isn't your concern. You are in the business of providing fabulous coffee and delicious food for them to "treat" themselves. If they want a health farm they should go to a health farm – it is not your responsibility. You are there to offer them **the ability to treat themselves** for a relatively small amount of money. It is your job to make them leave your shop a little happier and a little more perked up than they were when they arrived. A little stronger and able to face the day ahead or the long journey home. Don't lose sight of this.

Ultimately the customer that comes into your shop and leaves having had a delicious, perfectly made, cappuccino and a beautiful tasty brownie is happier than the one who left having just a cappuccino. Your job is to make them happy when they leave. If they're happy when they leave, they'll come back.

So make sure you keep asking them the obvious questions: "Would you like something to eat with that?"; "Would you like to have a piece of our fabulous coffee cake with your coffee?"; "Would you like a coffee after your sandwich and coke – I can take the money now and bring it across when you're ready?" You need to be careful that you're not falling into the "I'm being pushy" mindset because it simply isn't the case. You're just **making it easier** for the customer to have a great experience in your shop – which is exactly why you set it up in the first place!

Hugo – true story

We wanted to help an hotel business increase their coffee profits. Much of their coffee was brewed at a base station and transferred to other parts of the hotel for conference, meeting and restaurant needs. This system was operated on our advice as it maintained consistency and minimized waste. But we were missing a trick. We realized that some customers in the hotel were prepared to pay more for something a little bit special.

So we introduced four single origin coffees which were brewed in thermos flasks and marketed by describing their taste profiles. We had to have a good enough system to ensure they were correctly prepared, but as the staff began to see the benefits and the customers began to taste them, we found that we were selling an extra £200 of coffee per day with only a few minor operational issues to deal with. This experiment has been a great success and has added significantly to our customer's bottom line.

33. Sell more cold drinks

This is one you really need to grasp properly – it can make a huge difference to your bottom line. Just think about how important the drink you have is to the enjoyment of a meal if you don't believe us. **Upselling drink** is not aggressive selling, it is simply a good way to ensure that the customer has a more enjoyable meal. If we have a burger most of us will enjoy it more with a coke. Likewise a sandwich will be more enjoyable with a glass of mineral water. A steak will always taste better, in any sane opinion, with a glass (or heaven forbid two) of Burgundy. This is a fact and regardless of personal preferences you must get this fact into the mind of your serving staff. Stop treating the drinks as an afterthought.

Johnnie – true story

I took over a busy café a few years ago and we started the process of analysing the tills. One glaring issue we noticed was the fact that only 10% of customers purchased a soft drink with their lunch. We moved the position of the drinks cabinet and improved the selection. Additionally we made it a lot harder, but not impossible, to get free tap water.

Within two months we had changed the ratio to 75%, resulting in a huge difference to the bottom line profit.

You must view drinks as being as important as the food. All of our effort goes into the food but very often we simply ignore the drinks and just expect the customer to ask if they want something. You are leaving a LOT of money on the table if you don't have a clear policy and training in place to help maximise drink sales.

The issue of "tap water" is complex, but one thing is clear – **it is NOT free**. You have a wage to prepare the glass, water rates costs, a cost to produce ice and a cost to clean the glass again. Saying a point blank "No" to tap water is contentious and can be a stage too far for certain customers. One policy we use is to allow it but make sure the staff are trained to ask, "Would you like still or sparkling water?" when a customer asks for water, as opposed to asking if it is just tap water they want. We have measured the difference in sales and it is substantial and yet the customer does not feel bullied with this technique. Again this requires careful training.

You should, at the same time as you train staff to sell away from tap water, try training them to match food and drink items. As ever, let them use their own personal tastes to keep the pitch natural but help them along with suggestions. And always make sure all the staff have tried every drink. Recently we visited a potential client's café and ordered a ginger beer. When the waitress was asked if it was spicy we were met with the following response: "I don't know – they never let us try anything in here."

Hugo – true story

In the early days of selling espresso based beverages we sounded just like the dozens of other sales people telling potential customers how good we were. So we decided to stop telling and show them instead, and opened the country's first ever Coffee Training Centre. The objective of all our sales calls became to get customers and potential customers into the training centre so that we could let them taste fantastic coffee and show them how they could make fabulous tasting coffee for their own businesses. Almost nobody left a training session without buying. You can apply your own version of this facility in your business by using a sampling strategy.

34. Get your customer flow right

The customer flow, in all aspects of your business, is vital to your success, particularly if you operate a traditional counter service operation and not table service.

Time after time we find the easiest way to increase profits within coffee businesses is to pick apart the flow and ensure that the customer has a greater, more logical selection of food and drinks beside them the entire length of the queue.

For example at lunch you must ensure that if a customer is buying hot or cold food, you have provided easy access to a large selection of drinks. Providing trays within easy reach enables more food to be carried easily. You **must** make the process of buying easy. Too often it is made frustratingly difficult for the customer. Making trays hard to find and not restacking them, keeping drinks behind the counter, forcing the customer to ask the server, placing savoury food after sweet food and confusing the customer - these are all cardinal sins. If you frustrate or confuse the customer then he or she will buy less – it's as simple as that.

The **science of customer flow** is something that you must pay attention to and there are great lessons to be learnt from all the large chains. They play with flow and product placement and measure the results. Even if your format is different, you need to be out there observing other similar businesses and timing how long it takes their queues to flow in comparison to yours. There is a lot to be learnt from the supermarkets too in this respect.

You can have the greatest food in the world and the most delicious coffee, but if you provide a slow service then you will simply annoy the customer and they will visit elsewhere. After you have observed how other places operate then you need to sit and study your own service over a couple of days and analyse the differences. Then use the lessons you have learnt to speed up your own operation. This is even more critical in the To-Go part of an operation.

Society is used to instant gratification these days and you need to be aware of that. Too fat? Don't bother with the gym just get it sucked out! Can't afford to buy that new sofa? Don't worry, our new credit card can mean you will have it today! Hungry? We'll serve you a burger in two minutes and you won't even have to get out of your car! Dominos pizza created a huge and highly successful business, not by producing great pizzas, but simply by guaranteeing to get it to you quickly while it was still hot.

What this means is that your customer's attitude towards waiting is poor – they won't want to do it. So make it as easy and as quick as possible to sell them as much as possible. Time is not money. **Time is everything**.

Wake up to just doing it...
"100% of the shots you don't take don't go in."
Wayne Gretzky

35. Make it easy for the customer to buy

Far too many coffee businesses make the whole process of buying much too difficult. To avoid falling into this trap there are some simple facts that you mustn't ignore.

1. If you make it hard for the customer to buy then he won't. Customers are always more intimidated and worried about making a fool out of themselves than you might think.

2. Where possible don't make them have to ask – for anything. This means **training your servers** to offer continually (but in a non-aggressive way), ensuring your product is open and easily accessible with tongs (if you offer counter service) and that your menu and signage clearly tells them how to go about getting what they want.

3. Open fridges sell better than closed fridges, uncovered product (where possible considering hygiene regulations) sells better than covered product. Clearly named and priced product sells better than unnamed product. Do not assume that just because you know what an item is called that the customer will know and be comfortable enough to ask for "one of those".

Johnnie – true story

We used to run a hugely successful café within a retail chain. It was a stunning success on many levels and we really felt there was little we needed to do to improve it.

However, as part of the retail business, we used to be assessed regularly for a variety of industry awards. We had won a number of these awards for the retail operation but the cafés were always ignored and treated as an afterthought. The governing body was essentially controlled by retailers and they weren't quite sure how to deal with food operations. They suddenly realised that they should be putting together some scoring criteria for cafés too and hastily threw together some ideas based on how they scored the retail business, i.e. they applied retail rules.

With a suitable level of conceit we ignored these rules since we were doing so well and arrogantly assumed they didn't know what they were talking about in relation to the cafés. Subsequently we were marked down for not having clearly labelled traybakes and scones. Once more we laughed and scoffed at them until the next year when we realised that we were perhaps being a little silly and petulant and should put some cards on each product before the next assessment. After all, we could always take them down after they left. But complacency and laziness meant that we didn't bother and we left them up.

A few weeks later I was trawling through the till readings and realised that since we had named all the traybakes we had increased sales of these items by 6%. This equated to an overall increase in turnover of 1% over the year which, for a business of that size was quite substantial. An extra 1% for doing nothing more than spending thirty minutes typing up some cards.

There are two clear lessons from this.

1. Don't ever think you know it all and that you don't need to do anything more to improve.

2. Look to other industries for techniques and tips, particularly retailers. There are an awful lot of strategies that you can borrow from other businesses that most coffee shop owners wouldn't ever dream of applying.

36. Work out your lifetime customer value

One of the most valuable lessons to learn in business is the concept of "lifetime value". This is what a customer is worth to you over the average period of time that they stay loyal to you. It is enormously effective in terms of increasing your own and your staff's perception of **how valuable a customer is**.

Obviously different customers have different values, but you can still make a decent approximation. Let's assume you have a customer who buys his morning takeaway coffee from you every day and his lunch three days out of five. On average he spends £8 a day which is £24 a week. We'll allow him six weeks holiday, so that's £1,104 a year. If we assume that he stays with you for four years then this equates to a total value of £4,416. This gives you a very different perspective of how you need to treat him daily, and how much money you should be prepared to spend to attract him in the first place.

Every coffee or food business has different customer profiles but here are a couple of real life examples that can perhaps help to illustrate the point a little more clearly.

Johnnie – true story

I had a busy coffee bar a few years ago that was frequented by a mother and daughter for coffee on average four days a week. Often they would bring at least one of the daughter's pre-school children. Their average spend was approximately £11 and they had been visiting us in this same regular fashion for about three years. Using the same rule as my example on the previous page we can see that they had already contributed £6000 of turnover to the business.

There was no reason for them to go elsewhere as long as we kept them happy. But we didn't. We had a problem with the dishwasher and it meant that we often had some cups that weren't quite as clean as they should have been. I was busy (i.e. complacent and didn't have decent systems) and had taken my eye off the ball a little with this site. They complained to a member of staff about the cups and were given replacements and a vague apology.

But it happened again so they complained to the manager. She got the machine fixed but it was still creating the same problem. They complained again and when we still had the problem a few days later they left and took their business elsewhere. They are now £2000 a year customers for a client and friend of mine in a neighbouring town. My loss was his gain and he, to his credit, looks after them very well. He should do – the gross profit they provide helps to pay his mortgage for two months of the year.

This lesson is harsh but valuable. When your regulars come in, listen to them and act on what they say. If they aren't happy move heaven and earth to make sure you fix whatever it is that is making them unhappy. You have to start seeing them in terms of their lifetime value and yearly value and not just in terms of that unique sale.

Too often we just regard our regulars as part of the furniture and take them for granted. So why not walk up to a couple of them today and simply thank them for their custom and see if there is anything you can do better for them!

Hugo – true story

A little over ten years ago I had a customer with a chain of sandwich bar cafés who ran into some financial problems. Ultimately they did a deal with their creditors and we ended up taking quite a substantial loss. It was a difficult time for the customer and a difficult time for our growing business. I was cross and ranted and raved to my brother that I'd never do business with them again.

He listened quietly and then sat me down with a set of figures. He showed me how much gross profit we had made from the customer in the past and how much he predicted the customer would provide in the future. I calmed down.

That customer has since created some inspirational food and beverage businesses and we have supplied him with a lot of coffee. The loyalty we created by not making a huge fuss over the debt has benefited our business enormously and, needless to say, that customer wouldn't consider taking his coffee business elsewhere.

The twist in the story is that customer was Johnnie. Sometimes you need to sit back and look at the bigger picture in relation to your customers and sometimes you have to take the rough with the smooth. Never underestimate the long term value of a loyal customer. Your business should always be structured on this premise and not on the individual "quick buck" scenario.

37. Consider the sizes... carefully

We call this portion analysis, and it is a major opportunity for profit that is very often ignored by coffee operators. As with any cuisine, recipe is the key but many businesses make the mistake of ignoring the basic recipe when creating different sizes of coffee, particularly when they are selling sit-in and to-go coffee.

First things first though. **You need to offer two sizes these days** – it's important to increase that spend and many people want a larger drink, especially if they are taking it away. On average when testing, we have found that approximately 25% more customers will take the larger size. The profitability levels will vary from site to site but for one client this has produced an extra £50 of profit every week. That's £2,600 extra profit a year – for almost no effort.

Secondly, you must make sure the large drink (or in many cases the smaller one) tastes as good as it can be. Consider carefully coffee to water and milk ratios and how they will impact on that hook-and-addict strategy that will ensure a good regular customer. There is no point in gaining short term profits at the expense of your integrity towards selling delicious coffee.

Now for a bit of controversy... Refuse to serve extra large drinks and tell everybody you just can't get them to taste good enough. It will keep you one step ahead of the chains and that awful bucket of milk that is just so crude and generally tastes awful. We love this one with our quality coffee customers too because we can sell the Italian small cup culture which always tastes better... need we say more?

38. Make it accessible and open. Make it look great

For counter service operations we have proven, time and time again, both within our own businesses and for clients, that if you merchandise your food appealingly and in a bountiful easy-to-buy fashion **you will see sales increase**. Every time – without fail. Every single time.

Here is a simple test to try and help illustrate one aspect of this concept. The concept that bountiful food sells. Take a top selling item on a busy day and put out just one or two in your standard serving position. Monitor the daily sales. Now compare these sales to your average for that day. You will see a reduction in sales for this item.

This discipline of moving around product and monitoring sales from your till roll is one of the fundamental keys to making more money in your café. The Golden Rule for selling food however, is to display your produce so that it appears bountiful, attractive and appetising.

Obviously for table service operations this doesn't apply, but the mindset does. You should still be trying to sell as evocatively as possible through the menu **and** have as much food on display as possible to help tempt the customer.

Wake up to enjoying today's pressure

"One of the most tragic things I know about human nature is that all of us tend to put off living. We are all dreaming of some magical rose garden over the horizon instead of enjoying the roses that are blooming outside our windows today."

Dale Carnegie

39. Use your sign wisely. Spend money and make your shop look obvious

Many people regard the sign as an expensive afterthought, or worse, an ego trip. But overlook the value of quality and clear signage at your peril. Obviously for very long established sites in small communities it is less important but for the rest of us our customers will always be a mix of regular and new customers. Never underestimate how easy your shop is to just walk past and how confusing a sign that only has your business name on it is to passing customers.

It sounds daft, but we recently added the words **"coffee shop"** under the name on the sign of a new site that had been struggling, and placed a large image of a coffee cup on the window, and very quickly we saw an appreciable change in the sales. Many new customers told us that they simply didn't realise what we were selling and avoided the shop. To our eyes it was blindingly obvious that it was a café, but your view of your business is always dramatically different to your customers. Never forget that.

So be prepared to spend money on **good clear signage** with a clear indication of what you do on it. If you operate in the evening then it needs to be as bright as possible too. A golden rule is to make it twice as bright as your signage maker suggests.

Another little rule to be aware of with signage is the length of message that a customer can read. When driving past a sign a potential customer can only read a maximum of four words. If you use more than this you will simply confuse them and they won't be able to take it in.

Hugo – true story

I had a customer who produced great coffee and ran a wonderful business. But they were in a slightly odd location at the end of a busy road and sales were slow.

Their signage was dowdy and unclear. We redesigned the signage to clearly articulate exactly what they were doing and spent a little money on a "wow" design. It wasn't cheap but sales instantly increased by 10% and the sign was paid for in full within four months.

40. Get creative with signage

Following on from general signage is the use of A-frames outside on the pavement. Obviously there are certain legal restrictions here and many landlords aren't keen on them, but IF YOU CAN PUT THEM UP THEN MAKE SURE YOU DO. They provide an amazing opportunity to inform passing customers of your offer.

We have created flexible A-frame solutions for a client which are changed for breakfast, morning, lunch and afternoon-evening. They allow you to keep selling and enable you to clearly show items that will tempt that passing customer into your café.

Don't be afraid to use two signs if you have the space, but try and keep the message as clean and simple as possible. Nice clear product images and four to six words maximum allows the information to be easily taken in by a passing potential customer.

And once you have them inside, those customers who sit-in are a captive market for you. If they're sitting on their own or simply waiting for someone to join them then you need to subtly grab their attention and explain to them how your café operates. Table talkers can come in many different forms, from a simple printed sheet left on the table to laminated sheets in a variety of holders. We have used triangular holders with three different messages to great success in the past but these are bulky and can be "too much" for certain table sizes.

These messages keep reinforcing what a great place your café is and help to entice customers to return. Examples of what you should be telling them are (but by no means exclusively):

- Menus.
- Menus for different times of the day to help them understand that you are open in the evenings or on Sunday.
- The "story" behind various food items on your menu.
- The effort you go to in creating brilliant coffee.
- Awards you may have won - as long as they are relevant. The customer, for example, has little interest in a training award or hygiene awards. They are interested in the fact that you might have won best cappuccino in your local area, as this will help reinforce the fact that they made a good decision to visit your shop.
- Offers that you run.
- Information about products and offers that may not be relevant to them whilst they sit there but will sink into their subconscious. For

Wake up to vision...

"Leaders keep their eyes on the horizon, not just on the bottom line."

Warren D. Bennis

example, details about forthcoming events, special offers and important dates, such as Valentine's day or Mother's Day.

41. Avoid "sour faced hags"

The moment you sit down in front of a potential employee, you can **instantly grasp** whether they want to be in the service business or not. People come into the coffee shop business (and indeed all forms of catering with customer contact) for a couple of reasons:

1. Because they genuinely like the buzz and ever changing atmosphere of a coffee shop, they like meeting new people and like to talk to customers.

2. Because they are untrained in anything else and assume you need very little training to work in a coffee shop.

Within the second category exist the "sour faced hags", the bitter and twisted old bags who life has dealt a cruel hand of cards to. They have no interest in the buzz of your coffee shop and no interest in your customers. Everything you do is an inconvenience to them and you yourself are a first class conman simply because you own a business and they do not, so you are luckier than they are.

Johnnie – true story

I was recently in a smart coffee shop with my family and the family of a good friend. This was ostensibly an ice cream café so we were the exact target market. They had a child friendly menu. It was busy but not overly so. We went through the usual hassle of ensuring the children had what they wanted and that they wouldn't be resentful and do the "I wanted what he's having!!!!" when the food arrived. We were pleasant, polite and ordered as quickly as we could.

But the owner of the establishment had forgotten the "avoid sour faced hags rule" and had unfortunately employed one of these delightful people. It was a counter service operation and she glared at us the whole way along and every order we gave her was greeted without a smile.

Eventually we got our food and it was okay. The coffee in the shop is actually quite good and since the children were well behaved the logical idea was to take another ten minutes and have a coffee after our food. But we were all unanimous in the fact that we just wanted to get out. My friend uttered the immortal words "I'd actually love an Espresso but I refuse to talk to that 'sour faced hag' again".

So we left, and they lost all the high margin coffee sales. Doh!

42. Make the customers feel you care

Most customers, apart from a hardcore few, are simply too jaded to complain these days. Yet you really need to hear those complaints, particularly if you aren't going to be onsite all the time (and you're not are you?).

You need to have a decent feedback system such as comment cards with an incentive for completion included. It doesn't have to be much, but you do need something to encourage feedback. Very often we have simply used a "Free Meal for Two" draw on a monthly basis to entice customers to fill the cards in.

You also need to ensure that they feel comfortable enough to write openly and honestly. This means providing a locked box for the card to be inserted into and not making a customer hand the card to a member of staff who may, perhaps, have caused them a problem.

Wake up to your own valuable expertise...

"Experience is a good teacher, but she sends in terrific bills."

Minna Antrim

Finally, you need to make customers feel that you really **will** read their comments and that **what they say does matter to you**. Put a note on your box explaining that cards will be read twice daily at 12.00 p.m. and 5.00 p.m. by the manager or owner depending on your own circumstances. This makes it seem that you really do value their effort and honestly care about what they think.

43. Use the list – cheapest marketing you'll ever do

The importance of creating some form of list to mail to your customers cannot be over emphasised. A list allows you to mail out a newsletter, which can be cheaply and simply produced in-house, to keep your customers informed of what you are doing.

This helps to create a sense of "community" which is a very powerful and overlooked aspect of why people choose a regular coffee shop. It also allows you to let customers know about various changes to the menu, special events you are holding and, most importantly of all, you can include offers to draw those customers back at times when you are slack in the business.

You can **create and collect a list** in various ways depending on your style of business. As covered previously, comment forms are a great tool and have two benefits. They help to get you feedback on the business while you aren't there and also enable you to build a list very quickly.

Depending on the style of your business it is worth asking for as much information as possible on comment forms. Birthday and anniversary information allows you to promote these occasions and make the customer feel special.

And if you can, get customers email addresses and mobile phone numbers too. Emailing or texting is much cheaper and less time consuming than traditional mailing. Don't exclude all forms of traditional mailing though. Test all your options and see which works best for you.

If you don't want to provide a comment card you can still create a list simply by asking for customer's business cards for a special prize draw. Or by creating loyalty discount cards with a name and address section. Simple competitions asking for ideas for new menu items can generate lots of names.

But once you have the names keep the contact regular and always, **always** include an offer in your mailing. You need to be using this list to drag customers back at times they don't usually visit, or at quiet times in your shop.

44. Create a catering side to your business

This has to be one of the easiest and cheapest ways to expand your business. It may not be for everyone but you can do it at various levels and the **potential profits** are huge.

The great advantage of catering is that most of the work is generally done outside of normal business hours and rarely do you need to spend any extra money to gear up for it. It's usually very easy to promote too since you are likely to have a loyal (but hopefully lazy) customer base who would love to be able to eat more of your food at home or at a party.

Johnnie – true story

I had a single site coffee shop once that we managed to triple our profits with by creating a subsidiary catering business operating out of it. We were making a small profit of about £20K a year until we realised that lots of the local offices around us were marketing and PR companies. A very simple mailshot to these companies meant we started delivering sandwiches and interesting nibbles to them for meetings and client pitches. Price was of little concern to them as long as the product was good, a little unique and arrived on time. When they were pitching for large advertising contracts the last thing they worried about was paying a few extra pounds to the caterer. They needed reliability and a little controlled "wow factor".

A few leaflet drops followed and some sweet talking to the clients enabled us to expand and grow this part of the business very quickly. We made a few simple (and inexpensive) changes to the inside of the shop to facilitate this new business and by the end of the year had added £40K to the bottom line. One particular contract used to provide us with approximately £10K of net profit in the run up to Christmas alone.

45. Post the utility bills

You've been through your muffin training session **(number 16)** and made sure your staff know exactly how tough it is to make money, but sadly most employees have short memories and when it's not their money who can blame them. Ensuring they keep the **"it's about the money"** mantra in their minds is an ongoing process.

One of the most valuable ways to do this is to post up your utility bills somewhere obvious that they will all see them, a notice board for example. Let them see just how much money is going out on a daily basis. Post up a few monthly statements and take a few moments to show everybody just how large your meat/veg/ bakery bill is. Put up your weekly or monthly wage totals (not individually broken down obviously) and let them see this too.

It doesn't need to be relentless, but it's a useful way of keeping the control of costs at the forefront of their minds.

Wake up to not having all the answers...
"Leadership and learning are indispensable to each other."
John F. Kennedy

46. Incentives for saving money and making money

Sadly it's human nature to constantly be thinking "what's in it for me?" But you can, and should, use this to your advantage. So after all your training and utility bill posting, often the best way to get staff to really help you make profit is to create incentives. If you provide some incentive for actually saving money or even making more money, then you'll very easily be able to keep them focused on the problem.

Make sure your incentives are both for **saving money and making money**. Don't forget every pound is not equal **(number 17)** and you need the people who are using your systems every day to keep reporting back. They will notice a lot of things that you don't and you shouldn't underestimate just how much knowledge or how many ideas they have picked up in previous jobs that simply haven't occurred to you yet.

The way to operate incentives can vary and there are no hard and fast rules. You can offer an incentive for every idea (good or bad) just to keep the process going, but this is open to abuse so you must try and ensure that there are some basic rules covering the usage. But, as ever, if you complicate it too much you'll lose momentum and they simply won't bother with it.

Ideally you should reward the best suggestions every month with a decent cash bonus. Taking (tax paid) cash from your own pocket and handing it over works a **LOT** better than putting it through their wages. It is best not to award different sums of money for different ideas though, since this is open to resentment from the winners (or losers) in such a deal. The concept of "employee of the month" is flawed for coffee shops since it is so closely allied to the fast food industry which most coffee shop staff like to think they are above, or at least different from.

But if you're going to operate a system like this, then stick at it. It's a classic example of the type of great idea that many coffee shop operators pick up from a book (like this!) and then lose interest in after a few months. Like anything, it will take a bit of work and commitment to keep it going, but you could be surprised at some of the great suggestions you get, and operated properly it reaps great rewards simply because it shows the staff that you attribute some respect to their knowledge and intellect.

47. Get creative with your marketing and steal ideas from other industries

Within most industries, and the coffee shop market is no different, we tend to become "stuck" in the same model that all our competitors do. We all put our prices up at roughly the same time and we all tend to operate in roughly the same manner in terms of promotions.

Wake up when you have a bad week...

"Inside of a ring or out, ain't nothing wrong with going down. It's staying down that's wrong."

Muhammad Ali

It took Starbucks to come along and essentially reinvent this model. By creating a much better "experience" and a lot of wow factor they were able to **charge up to three times** what other coffee shops were charging for essentially the same basic products. Basically they borrowed from the "cool bar" model and created a hip place to hang out that didn't sell alcohol.

This type of thinking is hugely beneficial to creating clean air between you and your competitors. You need to keep looking around at what other businesses in general are doing and see if you can copy these ideas. Open all your "junk mail" and see if there are any compelling offers in there that could be applied to your café. Watch what retailers are doing around you. Watch the offers and layout in the big supermarkets and see what you can learn from them. Very often these large chains will have spent huge fortunes testing and developing marketing campaigns before they roll them out to the stores. You can be pretty certain that they work by the time they've reached your area, so look hard and dissect what it is that they are trying to do and ask yourself if it's possible to transfer the idea to your café.

Hugo – true story

I was working with a highly successful pub group and we had created a wonderful coffee offer for them. The staff were experts in producing high quality cocktails so understood at a very base level the concept of creating excellent coffee. They were highly motivated and within a short time were producing coffee of a very high standard. The bar was in a busy city centre site with fabulous views and had a lovely relaxing ambience that could work equally well at 10.00 a.m. on a Monday morning as it did at 10.00 p.m. on a Saturday night. It was also next door to a coffee chain and takeaway coffee sales were poor.

We simply didn't seem to be able to fully persuade the customers that they should be enjoying their speciality coffee in a bar instead of elsewhere. Takeaway sales needed a jolt. We came up with an experiment taking a leaf out of the retail book.

At the start of January, while all the local shops had January sales posters plastered on their windows, we decided to do the same thing. We offered a January takeaway coffee sale with all coffees at 49p. "Everything must ToGo". Sales went from 40 to 50 takeaway coffees per week to an incredible average of 1800 per week throughout January. After the sale ended they dropped to approximately 700 to 800 per week at the normal price.

So do try stuff – make sure the low cost ideas don't damage your brand by timing it strictly and communicating it well. If they succeed, tweak and repeat them. If they fail just shout, "Next".

48. Create a "bible"

It's boring and hard work but you must create an instruction manual with a clear indication of just what your employees should be producing and how they should be dealing with the customers. Despite your best efforts to keep telling them how hard it is to make money, you can rest assured that they will, on occasion, still decide that things are better "their way". They will decide to use their dear old grandma's lasagne recipe and not yours. They will decide that your scones should be a bit bigger because that's they way they like them or indeed they may even decide that the scones should be a bit smaller to help "save you money".

Of course, when you are designing your menu, with all the margin "stars" that you have slaved over, you will have designed it in a very specific way – a way that **helps you make money**. Well, this way needs to be put down in the "bible" that all staff are given when they arrive. Not only should this manual cover every aspect of how they deal with the customer, it must also contain a visual image of every regular item on the menu detailing how it should be prepared and presented.

Now this may seem like a lot of hassle, but you would be amazed at just how quickly you can put something like this together. It does NOT have to be pretty, but it does have to be clear. Crystal clear and written as if you were dealing with an eleven year old. The basics must be cast in stone and when you have completed your manual you then need to sit all your employees down and ensure they fully understand the concept of being flexible for the customer.

The last thing you need or want one of your employees saying is: "I'm not allowed to do that – it says so in the manual". You need to go through countless examples and scenarios so that they can understand that ultimately they need to use their common sense.

If a customer wants his cappuccino in a latte mug then give it to him. If a customer wants you to sing them a song then sing them a song if it makes them happy. But this approach requires a lot of training. Your staff will need to be constantly informed of exactly what your ethos is and where to draw the lines. Some customers will "try it on" (although always less than people think) and you need to make sure that you have made it clear how to deal with these situations.

49. Beware staff attitudes towards business ownership

In the wonderful idealistic world of many employees you are simply a cruel capitalist pig who preys on decent hardworking customers. You need to ensure that you root out this inherent problem at the interview stage and make very sure that you do not employ these people. **Ask searching questions** about previous employers to assess attitudes to business. If they seem to be relentlessly running down previous employers then it's highly likely that they aren't for you.

Ask where they like to eat themselves and see if you can identify any prejudices about certain types of food. For example, whilst we have nothing against vegetarians, indeed they can be very useful in certain types of cafés, you need to make sure they won't inflict their personal opinions onto your customers.

Wake up to people criticism ... they rain on your parade because they have none of their own ...

"Your own mind is a sacred enclosure into which nothing harmful can enter except by your permission."
Ralph Waldo Emerson

Johnnie – true story

I once had an employee who, when asked whether the chicken was fresh replied: "I don't know – I don't eat flesh of any kind".
Hardly conducive to a pleasant mental image of the chicken dish we had so carefully prepared.

I have also in the past had staff who felt it was their duty to berate customers if they wanted a bag for their sandwiches. "Do you really need it? These bags aren't biodegradable and are very wasteful" was one such memorable line.

In short, you need to focus in on their attitudes to food and service and try to identify their opinions on the type of business you are running.

It will pay in the long term.

50. Make a big deal of the big days

Never lose an opportunity to make a big deal of Christmas, Valentines Day, Mothers Day, Easter etc. At Easter produce a special Easter cake and use it to upsell. Make sure you have great mince pies at Christmas and make a **story** out of your own special recipe. Use these opportunities to upsell and make the customer feel great. Why not give a rose to every female regular who comes in on Valentines Day? **Do something different** but keep ramping up the loyalty and get the staff involved so that they understand that creating a special experience is a good thing to do.

If you operate in the evenings then make damn sure you have a Valentines night menu. This is a BIG spend night – don't lose out. Or even have a special Valentines menu for lunch. Something a little different. It keeps your business interesting for customers **and** staff.

51. Think wisely before you open your second shop

This is such an easy trap to fall into and one that we encounter every day both with clients and our own businesses. The relentless urge to feed the ego by expanding into new areas and new outlets can be very strong and yet it is very often a big mistake.

Opening a second shop requires a **vastly tighter business format** than you need for just one shop, especially if you are on-site every day. Very quickly you can end up spending large amounts of time travelling to and from your various locations which inevitably means you take your eye off the detail that made your first site so successful in the first place.

Johnnie – true story

Once, many years ago, I owned a brilliant little sandwich bar. I had a business partner and we were making a solid £45K a year. There were a lot of things we could do to expand this business in its existing location but our egos said "no, let's open another one". So that's what we did. We took out loans, signed leases and put down deposits. We signed agreements in our own names and made personal guarantees. We bought a new van. We worked very hard for a year and then sat back with our nicely massaged egos and looked at our profits.

> But, we'd taken our eyes off the profitability of the first shop since we didn't have good enough systems in place and consequently its profitability dropped a little to £30K. We didn't get the new one quite right since it took a while to build up a reputation and persuade our new customers how great we were, so we only made £15K there. Net result £45K and a whole host of new problems.
>
> We did have nicely massaged egos through, and people told us we were great for having such a "little goldmine". So it was okay, wasn't it? For the answer to this may I refer you to item number one!

Expanding into new sites can very often work, but only if you are really prepared and have fully exploited all the profit opportunities in your first site.

- Have you exhausted catering?
- Does your existing site run effortlessly without you being there?
- Do you use your lists properly?
- Are you open as often as you could be?
- Do you use all the marketing tricks in the bag?
- Have you utilised all available space on your current site?

If the answer to any of the above is "no" then you really need to make sure opening another site is not an ego based decision and that you will absolutely, definitely be better off with two sites and not just one.

52. Give a bit extra

This guide was supposed to be **52** ways to make more profit. But we're giving you one more. This is not some "ra ra" motivational nonsense about giving 110%. It's just a mindset about doing the best job you can and then sitting back and thinking:

"What else can we do for the customers?""What else would I want to see and experience?""What would make me think 'WOW, that's great – I'm going back there'?"

As ever, include your employees. They will have their own ideas about service, marketing and promotions, some of which they will have picked up from other cafés or restaurants. It will also make them feel "warm and fuzzy" about working somewhere that really cares about doing great stuff. That is valuable in itself.

So give the customer a surprise every so often. Hand out a few coffees without forcing them to have full loyalty cards. Make an effort to be a little bit more friendly than the competition. Give out a few free portions or hand out taster samples of new products. Spend a little longer genuinely trying to learn about their lives in your chats with them. Provide a wider range of magazines and papers to read. Allow free wireless internet access. Whatever works for you and your business. **But keep at it and keep surprising them.**

53. Work "on" the business not "in" it

This is the biggie – this is your big extra one. When we were kids and got a new book, most of us probably loved to go straight to the back page and see what happened at the end of the story. To see the happy ending.

So that's why we put this one here – because it's **so important**. And it is a happy ending because it's about helping you to **make money** even when you're not there.

It's almost as important as our **it's all about the money** rants. You are not a cook or a fancy chef or a till assistant – you are a business person. That doesn't mean that you can't serve any customers or make the odd cake, but

Wake up to working on the most important thing …
"Once you have a clear picture of your priorities- that is values, goals, and high leverage activities- organize around them."
Stephen Covey

you have to shift at least a part of your day to the process of running the business – of working "on" and not "in" your business.

What happens to most people who open almost any food business is that they have a dream of being able to cook "full-time" or "serve lovely food" rather than have to put up with the tedium of their previous daily job. This misguided notion is often converted into a strong conviction by a few well meaning guests at dinner parties they hold at home.

Subsequently off they go to remortgage the house and open a nice little coffee shop. With no real concept of running it like a business and no idea how to create systems for controlling cashflow, finance, staff, and product quality, they fling the doors open to their fictional paradise which quickly turns into their biggest nightmare.

Another scenario is the chef who has cooked all his life in a professional kitchen but is now desperate to do it "himself". Of course he is no more qualified than the previous example and is basically just the same as the plumber who decides he should open a large plumbing business, just because he's good at fixing toilets. **Running a coffee shop is about running a business**. It is not some idealistic dream of having people pop round for coffee with you and paying for the privilege. You need to get solid systems in place to deal with your staff. You need to develop training programs and, more importantly, stick with them. You need a marketing plan and a decent grasp of accountancy so that you don't end up sitting on the street after 18 months of huge slog with debts so large that it will take you the rest of your life to pay them off.

Wake up to what you don't know ...

"The problem with most failing businesses is not that their owners don't know enough about finance, marketing, management, and operations - they don't, but those things are easy enough to learn - but that they spend their time and energy defending what they think they know. My experience has shown me that the people who are exceptionally good in business aren't so because of what they know but because of their insatiable need to know more."

Michael Gerber

So get out of the kitchen and away from the till, and run it like a business! And if you need help then **give us all call** and we can maybe make it a little easier for you.

And finally...

So there they are. 52 ways to make more money out of your coffee business with one more thrown in for good measure. As we said at the start, our purpose was not to create an exhaustive manual or a dry textbook for running your business.

We have deliberately used a light-hearted approach, but please don't confuse this tone with frivilous content. The "52 ways" concept is deliberately structured to allow you to take small actions every week.

There is, hopefully, no need to redesign your business from scratch, so why not take the top five tips that resonated most with you and apply them over the next five weeks. Take simple actions that shouldn't put your business under too much strain. Then measure the results and maybe tweak a few things. And then apply another five.

The important thing is to **do something**. The secret is not in the knowing but in the doing. Don't just read the book and nod knowledgably and then simply go straight back to your normal working pattern. Nothing will change unless you make it change.

Wake up to action ...

"To know and not to do is not yet to know."

The 14th Dalai Lama

And don't forget, if you need help then please get in touch.

Thanks

It's something of a cliché when writing a book to go into great detail about how impossible it would have been without the help of a huge range of people. Now that we have finally written our book we realise just how true this is.

A huge number of people have been immeasurably helpful to both of us during our careers and globally we would like to thank them all for their assistance. They know who they are and rather than offend any individuals we don't want to indulgently list out every name.

Specifically, in terms of the production of this book, it genuinely wouldn't have been possible without the tireless efforts of Lesley Allen, Stuart Kennedy, Darren Rooney, Nick Moffat and Julia Stewart. And, of course, the little man with the cheap brown suit.

More from
The Coffee Boys

Seminars, Training Programmes, Conferences, Speaking Engagements and Events

For further information contact:

The Coffee Boys
Coffee House
5 Shandon Drive
Ballyholme
Bangor
BT20 5HL

E john@thecoffeeboys.com
W www.thecoffeeboys.com

Would you like lots of FREE stuff?

Pop along to www.freecoffeeboys.com and you'll find lots of free content to hopefully inspire you within your business.

Amongst other goodies you'll be able to

- View a free video of our key note speech "Ten Ways to Beat the Credit Crunch"
- Watch regular interviews with industry and marketing experts
- Get advance notification of when and where we are next speaking
- Watch the legendary "Ten commandments" videos
- Download various articles and audio

24123772R00072

Made in the USA
San Bernardino, CA
12 September 2015